Rookie Read-About® Science

Gator or Croc?

By Allan Fowler

Consultants

Linda Cornwell, Learning Resource Consultant,
Indiana Department of Education

Fay Robinson, Child Development Specialist

Lynne Kepler, Educational Consultant

ℙ Children's Press®
A Division of Grolier Publishing
New York   London   Hong Kong   Sydney
Danbury, Connecticut

Project Editor: Downing Publishing Services
Designer: Herman Adler Design Group
Photo Researcher: Caroline Anderson

Library of Congress Cataloging-in-Publication Data

Fowler, Allan.
    Gator or croc? / by Allan Fowler.
      p. cm. – (Rookie read-about science)
    Includes index.
    Summary: Simple text and illustrations describe the differences
between alligators and crocodiles.
    ISBN 0-516-20027-5 (lib. bdg.) — ISBN 0-516-26080-4 (pbk.)
    1. Alligators—Juvenile literature. 2. Crocodiles—Juvenile literature.
[1. Alligators. 2. Crocodiles.] I. Title. II. Series.
QL666.C925F68   1996
597.98—dc20   96-13226
                                                            CIP
                                                            AC

You know what this fierce–
looking reptile is — an alligator.

Or is it a crocodile?
Here's a quick way
to tell the difference.

If several of its lower teeth are sticking out when the animal has its jaws closed . . . then it must be a crocodile.

crocodile

alligator

When an alligator's jaws
are closed, you can't see
any of its lower teeth.

crocodile   alligator

Also, a crocodile's snout
comes to more of a point
than an alligator's snout.

Both crocodiles (crocs) and
alligators (gators) stay in
the water much of the time.

alligator

Their long tails whip back and forth, helping them to swim fast.

crocodile

crocodile

Their nostrils and eyes are on top of their heads, so they can breathe and see above water while swimming.

9

But they can stay under water a long time without breathing — as much as an hour for larger crocodiles and alligators.

alligators

They live only in places
that are usually warm.

Alligators are found along
the Atlantic coast of the
United States, from North
Carolina to Florida . . .

and in all the states along
the Gulf of Mexico.

alligator

There are alligators in China, too.

Crocodiles live in the Americas, Africa, Asia, and Australia.

Alligators and crocodiles belong to a family of reptiles called crocodilians.

There are two other
kinds of crocodilians —
caimans, in Central
and South America . . .

caimans

gavials

and gavials, in India.

alligator

An alligator might
be about 15 feet long,
but most are smaller.

Some crocodiles have
been known to reach
20 feet or more.

Leathery skin, with thick plates called scales, covers the bodies of crocodilians.

alligator skin

crocodile toes and claws

Their toes are webbed, and
they have claws on their feet.

A female lays dozens of eggs at a time, about the size of chicken eggs.

Baby gators or crocs are
only 8 to 10 inches long.
But they grow fast — about
a foot each year for 3 or 4
years, then more slowly.

baby alligators on mother's back

Crocodiles and alligators like to lie motionless in the sun for long hours.

crocodile

alligator with fish

They often hunt for food
at night. They eat fish and
shellfish, birds and mammals,
turtles and frogs.

alligator

The croc or gator uses
those strong jaws and
sharp teeth to grip its prey.

It can stun an animal with
one swipe of that long tail.

alligator

Alamosaurus   crocodilian

Alligators and crocodiles are thought to live as much as 100 years or more in the wild.

And they have been around longer than most animals.

When dinosaurs walked the earth, they had crocodilians as neighbors.

Yet, human beings came close to killing all the alligators and crocodiles in our country.

Now, laws protect those remarkable creatures.

Crocs and gators deserve to be studied and admired.

But please admire them from a safe distance!

crocodile

Words You Know

Crocodilians

alligator

crocodile

caimans

gavials

nostrils eyes

snout   teeth

claws toes   scales

Index

Alamosaurus, 26

alligators (gators) and crocodiles (crocs)

   babies, length and growth, 21

   breathing, 10

   claws, 19, 31

   difference between, 3, 4, 5, 6

   eggs, 20

   eyes, 9, 31

   feet, 19

   food eaten, 23

   hunting, 23

   jaws, 4, 5, 24

   laws protecting, 28

   length of life, 27

   length of (size), 16, 17

   nostrils, 9, 31

   scales, 18, 31

   skin, 18

   snout, 6, 31

   tail, 8, 25

   teeth, 4, 5, 24, 31

   toes, 19, 31

   where they live, 11, 13

caimans, 14, 30

   where they live, 14

crocodilians, 13, 14, 15, 18, 26, 27, 30

dinosaurs, 27

gavials, 15, 30

   where they live, 15

prey, 24

reptile, 3, 13

swimming, 8, 9

water, 7, 10

About the Author

Allan Fowler is a free-lance writer with a background in advertising. Born in New York, he lives in Chicago now and enjoys traveling.

Photo Credits

Photo Researchers Inc. — ©Tom McHugh, cover, 6 (left), 19, 29, 30 (top right), 31 (bottom left); ©David R. Perdew, 6 (right), 30 (top left); ©Root/Okapia/PR, 8; ©M.P. Kahl, 9; ©James Rod/National Audubon Society, 20; ©J.H. Robinson, 21

SuperStock International, Inc. — ©Gary Neil Corbett, 3; ©Gerard Fritz, 26

Valan Photos — ©Robert C. Simpson, 4, 31 (top); ©Arthur Strange, 7; ©Jeff Foott, 10; ©Stephen J. Krasemann, 12, 25; ©Francis Lepine, 14, 30 (bottom left); ©Wayne Lankinen, 16-17; ©Phillip Norton, 18, 31 (bottom right); ©Joyce Photographics, 22

Visuals Unlimited — ©Tom J. Ulrich, 5, 23; ©Ken Lucas, 15, 30 (bottom right); ©David G. Campbell, 24

COVER: Saltwater crocodile, Thailand